# Maud Humphrey:

## Her Permanent Imprint
## on American Illustration

# Maud Humphrey:
## Her Permanent Imprint
## on American Illustration

Schiffer Publishing Ltd
77 Lower Valley Road, Atglen, PA 19310

## Karen Choppa & Paul Humphrey

**Maud Humphrey:**
**Her Permanent Imprint**
**on American Illustration**

Copyright © 1993
by The Balliol Corporation

ISBN: 0-88740-540-1 (hard cover)
ISBN: 0-88740-546-0 (soft cover)
Library of Congress Number 93-85279

Published by Schiffer Publishing Ltd.
77 Lower Valley Road
Atglen, PA 19310
Please write for a free catalog.
This book may be purchased
from the publisher.
Please include $2.95 postage.
Try your bookstore first.

We are interested in hearing from authors with
book ideas on related subjects.

## Acknowledgements

The authors wish to thank the following individuals:
  Gwen Goldman for supplemental Maud Humphrey
    artwork;
  Anne Elisabeth Martin, granddaughter of Maud
    Humphrey's cousin, Bertha Humphrey Nolan;
  Marvin Mitchell for his support, research assistance,
    and commitment to publicizing the often-overlooked
    contributions of women illustrators;
  Joanne Pickering, our California "detective," for her
    research work;
  Sarah Steier for supplemental Maud Humphrey art-
    work;
  John D. Williamson, grandson of Maud Humphrey's
    cousin, Lillian Humphrey Williamson.

In addition, the following organizations aided in research
  for this project:
  The Balliol Corporation for the bulk of the Maud
    Humphrey images found in this book;
  The Landmark Society of Western New York;
  The Memorial Art Gallery;
  The Rochester Historical Society;
  The Rochester Museum and Science Center;
  The Rochester Public Library;
  The University of Rochester Library.
A special thank-you is extended to the City of Rochester
  for its warm hospitality.

# Contents

VIOLET

COPYRIGHTED

This Maud Humphrey image appeared in sepia on the cover of *The Post Express* Art Supplement, March 26, 1896, in Maud's hometown of Rochester, New York. The hand coloring was done by a contemporary Rochester artist years later.

# *Preface*

Maud Humphrey was one of the most popular illustrators in America at the turn of the century. Unfortunately, history, while it has a way of molding characters, also has a way of eclipsing their contributions. Through the years, Maud's impact on American illustration had been lost. To recent generations it seemed her only claim to fame was as the mother of Hollywood legend Humphrey Bogart. However, Maud's role on the American art scene was as remarkable as any role her son ever played on stage or screen, her popularity in her day as intense as any Bogie cult following.

Today, there is a resurgence of interest in Maud Humphrey's work. A growing interest in her life and the forces that shaped her career have prompted this book. It is a look at a young woman growing up in Victorian times, the mark those times left upon her outlook and values and the limitations those times set before her. Women of the "genteel set" were limited to careers in art, teaching, writing and nursing. They were still not accepted in the "professions," and factory work was deemed "outside the pale of polite society."

Maud Humphrey took that limitation and made it work for her, and she went beyond many of the other limitations that Victorian times generated. She became an early suffragette and maintained her art career even after marriage and a family. Throughout this book the artist is referred to as Maud Humphrey, the professional name she chose to use, rather than her married name of Bogart.

*Maud Humphrey: Her Permanent Imprint on American Illustration* looks at the various factors that created this successful artist, this strong character. Beyond the inborn talent there was the cultural upbringing in a well-to-do neighborhood, the historical advances being made in art publication, and the social attitudes of and towards women as the Victorian era came to a close.

This book is a joint effort between two writers. One, a second cousin to Maud Humphrey, has added his personal insight and recollections of Maud Humphrey and of Rochester, New York, where they both grew up. His contributions are highlighted throughout the book in Italics. The other has added the facts and events of Maud's lifetime as they have been uncovered in hours of research. Many events have been lost forever, like so many of the artist's original paintings and sketches. The facts that are known point to a life filled with professional successes and personal tragedies, to a complex woman who courted contradiction. Many of the Maud Humphrey images that do remain grace these pages. Black-and-white border designs by her sister Mabel Humphrey (Green) from children's books illustrated in color by Maud and written by Mabel are interspersed throughout the biography.

A biography is what this book is intended to be, not a complete works catalog. The illustrations within are just a sampling from Maud Humphrey's voluminous works. She did illustrations for a number of books including *Babes of the Nation, Baby Folk, Baby Sweethearts, Baby's Record, Bonnie Little People, Book of Fairy Tales, Children of the Revolution, Cosy Time Sto-*

*ries/Storybook, Favorite Fairy Tales, Favorite Rhymes, Gallant Little Patriots, Golf Girl, Light Princess, Little Colonial Dame, Little Grown-Ups, Little Heroes and Heroines, Little Homespun, Little Soldiers, Littlest Ones, Make-Believe Men and Women, Mother Goose, Old Youngsters, Poems, Rosebud Stories, Sleepy Time Stories, A Treasury of Stories, Jingles and Rhymes,* and *Two Valentines.* Many of these illustrations appear again on calendars, postcards, and advertisements.

Like the numerous errors previously printed about Maud and her career, there are many images attributed to her that are in dispute. The authors have chosen not to use any images in question among the illustrations for this book and acknowledge that additional Humphrey works continue to come to light.

"Her First Ball" from *The Littlest Ones* was translated into a figurine, "My First Dance," ninety years later.

## CHAPTER ONE
# *Portrait of an Artist*

We can turn to photographs and a self-portrait for a visual glimpse of the artist Maud Humphrey. However, it is the descriptions in clippings and articles and recollections of her son, Humphrey Bogart, that give us a more detailed impression of Maud. Reading between the lines tells us about her personality, as well as her physical appearance.

The strongest memory of a young Paul Humphrey was of Maud's size as she loomed over him as she patted his shoulders. Her size and enthusiasm made Maud's pat on the shoulders more like a resounding whack.

*There was nothing "petite" about Maud, as one writer deduced from a faded photograph, more faded than realized. She was a big woman, about five feet ten inches tall, with frizzy hair occasionally pampered with early versions of permanent wave. Her features, front focus, were even and winsome, as in her self portraits, but profiles show a firm jaw and sizable nose. Her hands were small, and her feet, a source of inordinate vanity, a size 2 1/2, hardly sufficient to balance their*

*regal proprietor. One of her delights was the salesman's incredulous comments whenever she stopped at a proper dispenser of bootery.*

*It can be assumed that as a child she was bundled up in the fulsome frocks, prissy petticoats and colorful outers so often portrayed in her paintings.*

*Play clothes they were not; in her circle, little girls were discouraged from vigorous sports. Such activities were considered unseemly and dangerous.*

*In her adult and professional life, her wardrobe, at least in public, was individual - almost bizarre. With the white or light gray and mauve colors she preferred, her clothes were a symbol, almost a signature. In an extended interview with her son, Humphrey, these singularities were described in detail. Bogart's first impression of his mother was white rubber boots. In wet weather there was also a white rain coat and even taller boots, about the same height as her then two-year-old wondering namesake. All this was adorned with a lavender scarf flourish.*

*No country girl, Maud wore citified costumes wherever she was: high heels, lace chokers, bright bows and rainbow ribbons, all on an hourglass figure. At the summer place in Canandaigua, New York, she sported an elaborate silk bathing suit, but never got wet, the true "darling daughter." These whimsies and attitudes earned her the sobriquet "Lady Maud" which she lived up to the hilt.*

*For no known reason, Maud hated hats, though flowery toppers were featured in much of her artistry. She owned only one, a dingy black nothing kept handy for functional purposes.*

*In her studio she donned crisp smocks while working, often standing up. In later life she lost her interest in theatrical trappings and retreated to simple, impeccable skirts and blouses. Whatever and wherever, she was always neatly and fashionably dressed with, as in her artwork, a style all her own.*

It has been said of "Lady Maud" that, "beautiful, stately and fastidious, she looked and acted the part." She had a presence about her that commanded respect and likewise thwarted closeness. Even her children called her "Maud." This was one of the many seeming contradictions in her life. The story-book images she painted were full of sentiment and warmth, but she seemed to look upon emotion in real-life relationships as unnecessary clutter.

*Though she maintained satisfactory relationships with professional associates, her caustic wit and imperious manner discouraged suitors and limited other relationships. She had no close friends and avoided most occasions where her pictures or presence were not admired.*

This lack of emotional attachment seemed to enable Maud to concentrate on her artwork with her total being. She was devoted to her work, yet she was also strongly motivated by her Victorian sense of duty to her family. The two goals were entwined. Her dedication to her career enabled her to provide well for her family, and her family's dependence on her drove her to succeed.

*Work was her fulfillment, her religion, her life. Some unaccountable force drove this young girl, successful adult, wife and mother to creative efforts almost beyond belief. She limited her sleeping time to five hours a night, and the number of her renditions ran into the thousands.*

Hence another contradiction, this between Maud's upbringing and her subsequent career. Her own mother had been typical of the wives and mothers of that

**Opposite page:** Self-portrait of Maud Humphrey.

social class and time. Mostly "decorative," their functions centered on social activities and "hobbies." That Maud chose a career was foreign to her background, that she continued that career in the face of marriage and raising a family was foreign to the times. Yet her upbringing remained a crucial element in her life.

*Consciousness of her connections and background was one of Maud's most sustaining, and sustained, characteristics. She often mentioned her prominent family, exclusive residence and professional associations, and pride in her origins was evidenced by the use of her maiden name signatures and the "Humphrey" in Humphrey Bogart.*

This was part of the conservative side of Maud, the "sense of duty" side. For the most part, her politics were conservative, too. Still, and herein lies yet another contradiction, Maud was a leader in the early suffragette movement. Undoubtedly she had met fellow Rochesterian Susan B. Anthony along the way. Maud believed strongly in equal rights for women, in the homes, as well as at the polls, and she practiced what she preached. One of her last public acts was participation in a strike demonstration by women workers.

In the end we have a portrait of a complicated individual, "individual" being the key word here. There was no pigeon-holing Maud Humphrey. A "conservative Bohemian"...a career artist juggling home and family...a no-nonsense woman painting sentimental scenes. But what of the palette and brush strokes that created that portrait? What of the events in her life that fashioned Maud Humphrey from a young girl growing up in the affluent Third Ward of Rochester, through studies in Paris, to a successful art career in New York City, to becoming a Hollywood matriarch?

"Springtime Gathering" painted by Maud Humphrey in 1889 and published by Frederick Stokes. The same image appears in black and white as the frontispiece for *A Treasury of Stories, Jingles and Rhymes.*

# CHAPTER TWO
## A "Ruffled Shirt" Heritage

Rochester, New York, has been known as both the Flour City and the Flower City. It was once the capital of the flour industry. In 1882, when the eastern section of the Erie Canal was completed and the first boat carrying flour left Rochester for Little Falls, the former already had five flour mills in its midst. The Canal brought a new outlet for distribution, and the growth of the flour industry began in earnest. In 1860, Rochester was still the Flour City and had twenty-one mills, but in the years that followed midwestern cities closer to the great grain-producing areas began to surpass Rochester. By 1878, the flour industry in Rochester had passed its peak.

Nurseries took over where the mills left off, retaining for Rochester a reputation and a favorable trade balance. Now the *Flower* City, its streets were a maze of trees and flowers, the plantings of many nurseries. There were acres of tulips and seemingly endless rows of young fruit trees. This was the Rochester in which Maud Humphrey grew up.

While it was still a young mill town, the Third Ward became the home of Rochester's elite. Nathaniel Rochester himself set the style when he built his home at Spring and Washington Streets. The Third Ward consisted of a triangle bound by the Erie Canal on the North, the Genesee River on the East, and the Genesee Valley Canal on the West. These "moats" set the Third Ward apart onto itself. Within this isolation a certain lifestyle evolved.

Rochester, New York, was originally known as the Flour City for its many mills and later as the Flower City for its numerous nurseries.

*Beginning in the 1830s, wealthy manufacturers, merchants and prominent professionals gathered on these grounds. Their owners were men of ambition and substance. They considered themselves a selected vintage and fulfilled their conceptions of value by manners and manors, thus founding a classic commune and self-glorified aristocracy.*

*In time this exclusive enclave acquired the title of "The Ruffled Shirt District," inspired by the fluffy frontage of white shirts worn with formal jackets, the rest of the garment sedately out of sight. Flaunting this fancy credential was a bit of "side" practiced by those so distinguished. It is true that on one occasion, while folks rocked serenely in wickers set out on verandas, a brash householder shed his jacket right out there in the open. Within minutes the porches were emptied, and rocking chairs teetered and stalled in disburdened futility. The author of this outrage repaired his bloodied repute by emphatic apologies. Even a much regarded judge was not above inadvertently parting his judicial vestures to brandish a glimpse of his opulent finery.*

Maud's paternal grandfather, Harvey Humphrey, was one such "much regarded judge." His home had been pioneer Enos Stone's house, "the first mansion built in Rochester on the East side of the River." The Humphrey lineage also included a lawyer uncle and a cousin whose rare bookstore in the Third Ward was nationally known and lent an erudite air to the neighborhood.

On her mother's side, Maud's grandfather, Henry Churchill, was a successful businessman in shoe manufacturing. This industry was a dominant force in Rochester during the 1860s, greatly stimulated by Civil War contracts. Eventually the firm of Churchill and Company employed 600-800 men with a trade of $1,000,000 a year. In keeping with his standing, Henry Churchill was Director of the City Bank and an elected Elder of Central Presbyterian Church. And in keeping with his standing, he, too, took up residence in Rochester's Third Ward.

Here, in the environment of the prestigious Third

Poster for the nationally-known bookstore of George P. Humphrey, Maud's cousin.

Ward, Maud completed her transformation from girl to young woman. She had been born across the river on the corner of North Washington and Main Street on March 30, 1868. (Today, an art supply store occupies that site as though Maud's muse still lingers there.) From there, the family had moved briefly to Frank Street. In 1884, Maud along with her father, mother, and sister moved in with Maud's maternal grandparents at 3 Greenwood in the Third Ward (later renumbered to 5 Greenwood).

Greenwood is in a particular section of the Third Ward known as the Corn Hill neighborhood, because here was once a hill crowned by fields of corn. As well as ending up as corn meal, the grain had also been used as fodder for pigs that became the once-famous brand of Corn Hill hams and bacons. Today the area is a preservation district where 5 Greenwood still stands.

The last corn had been harvested by the time Maud and her family moved into the Third Ward. Stately homes and mansions had replaced the corn fields. These older homes with their vaulted ceilings, crystal chandeliers, and wide, carpeted stairways were built for "large families, comfortable living, and lavish entertaining." Near 5 Greenwood, and towering over most of the Third Ward, was the "Kimball Castle." William S. Kimball, a tobacco magnate, owned all of Troup Street from Greenwood to Clarissa. His mansion on the hill at Troup and Clarissa housed a private art gallery, an orchid house, a music gallery with a pipe organ, and stables filled with thoroughbred horses. Louis Comfort Tiffany had designed the entire interior, from iron grillwork to the draperies.

Not all homes in the Third Ward were as large or as extravagant. Merchants, craftsmen, and millers lived side-by-side with politicians and professionals. The brick-and-flagstone sidewalks led equally from mansions to cottages to Rochester's first row-type housing. No matter the residence, however, the manner and bearing were

Scene with Maud Humphrey's birthplace in the background.

the same, for each Third Warder was proud of his neighborhood and the social customs inherent therein. The Ward was more than a geographic location, it was a "state of mind" where residents of a bustling city went about their daily affairs with village-like gentility.

Social functions flourished within the Third Ward. Livingston Park was the heart of the Ward, a private parkway maintained by abutting property owners. The gates to the narrow roadway were usually closed every evening and Sabbath, but there were many times when they remained open as Third Warders gathered on the green at Livingston Park for community suppers, band concerts and prayer meetings.

Throughout the year there were tea parties, going-away and coming-home parties, theatricals and charades,. In the spring there were the drives into the country to pick flowers for May baskets to be hung on neighbors' doors. In late summer the air was filled with the aromas of pickling and preserving as neighbors went from home to home sharing their garden harvests. Everything from rhubarb to mincemeat filled the pantries. In the fall, Halloween celebrated with enthusiasm. knew a wilder-cret shortcuts fences and swinging and was much The children ness of se-over picket through the alley gates, the area's shady streets, broad lawns, and well-kept gardens made grand hiding places. In the winter, there were get-togethers after sleigh riding or bobsledding on Troup Street hill. The Erie Canal, which was drained for the winter from Exchange Street to South Av-

enue, was flooded to provide the perfect skating rink. To begin the cycle again in the finest fashion, there were open houses on New Year's Day when visits were made or calling cards left.

Clubs thrived in the Third Ward's atmosphere, offering even more social functions. Maud herself joined the Rochester Art Club in its infancy. Her paternal grandfather, Judge Humphrey, was a founding member of the Pundit Club, a group that met to discuss science and literature.

The Third Ward, this choicest of Rochester's residential districts, was separated from the business district by the Erie Canal. It was a comfortable distance for the businessmen and professionals living in the Third Ward, like Maud's father who had his store on State Street. The heart of this business center was the "Four Corners."

*Though not a physical part of the Third Ward, Rochester's "Four Corners" was, and in part still is, the center of the City's professional and business activity, located at the junctures of Main (once called Buffalo) Street, State and Exchange.*

*Three classic buildings graced this hub. First was the Reynolds Arcade, a spectacular piece of architecture and a principle City "sight." It was 100 feet wide and 135 feet long, though it was later extended. The lower floor was lined with shops, art galleries, eateries, and two barber shops. On the upper levels were offices of the better sort.*

*Gracing Main and State Streets was the mighty Powers Building, largely an office complex, but better known as a show place and recreational Mecca, with several extensive art galleries, ball rooms, lounges, conference facilities, and a small theater. For pow-wow or tete-a-tete, Powers was the place. Some time later a tower was added.*

**Opposite page:** A scene of the residences flanking Livingston Park in the Third Ward.

Early downtown Rochester, New York, in the horse-and-buggy days of Maud's youth.

*That brings one to the Wilder Building, on the corner of Main and Exchange Streets. This locale was much favored by lawyers. Squared, red and forthright in design, it was higher than the Powers Building. After that came the tower of Powers, and so the affront was mended.*

These buildings, and the "Four Corners" in general, were important aspects of Third Ward life. Whether by foot or horse-drawn carriages, Third Warders made their way across the hump-backed draw bridges over the canal to work, shop, or play there. The Powers Building was the sight of many balls and parties where the elite mingled with the season's debutantes, or "buds" as they were called. A balcony extended the entire way around the Mirror Hall in the Powers Building enabling the dowagers to sit and keep tabs on activities on the dance floor. A climb to the top of the tower revealed a panoramic view of Rochester, including the Third Ward, looking like an island of leafy green with all its trees pierced by the steeples of First Presbyterian and Plymouth Church.

The first Western Union telegraph office was in the Reynolds Arcade which for years would remain the telegraphic center of America. The Reynolds Arcade also housed the Post Office from 1833 to 1891. So it was a center of communication and socializing. On Sunday mornings after church, crowds of men in bowler hats and cutaway coats stopped by there for their mail. Then it was back home again across the canal to their Third Ward retreat and Sunday dinners of soup, chicken with all the trimmings, topped off with wine jelly and whipped cream. Afterwards some napped while others sat on porch steps exchanging greetings with fellow Warders.

If Maud Humphrey kept a diary of her early teens years in the Third Ward it has been lost to us now. However, it isn't hard to imagine her standing on the hump bridge at Washington watching the canal life

The Rochester Savings Bank where the Rochester Art Club met.

The prominent Powers block, housing a hotel, offices, and an art gallery.

below her. The children delighted in the long, flat canal boats where housewives knitted in rocking chairs in the deck house doorways and drying wash fluttered from the deck. Across, the bridge Maud would have seen the plodding mules pulling the canal boats and, beyond the towpath, the tree-lined streets of her Third Ward.

It's almost certain she would have visited the Powers Art Gallery in the Powers Building drawn there by her love of art and to add to her own art instruction. Daniel W. Powers traveled abroad collecting art objects. The upper suite of rooms in the Powers Building became the permanent home for his growing collection. At one point that collection contained 1000 paintings and 17 pieces of statuary, and the gallery was considered the finest in America. It is even likely that Maud's own artwork found its way into that gallery before the collection was broken up upon Mr. Powers's death in 1897.

Did she herself go to the Reynolds Arcade to collect the mail with the envelope telling her she had been accepted for study at the Art Students League in New York? One can only guess, but certainly Maud knew the old Arcade well. There was an artists' corner there among the galleries where she could watch brushes and palettes in action.

She would have come into the "Four Corners" on her way to the Rochester Savings Bank where she would meet with other members of the Rochester Art Club. The building with its elevators like gilded bird cages and offices with 15 foot ceilings and fireplaces provided the right aesthetic atmosphere. The "Four Corners" too was the hub of the horse-drawn streetcar lines which Maud would have ridden about the city.

*The decade of the 1880s witnessed the full flowering of the Third Ward as the quintessence of social sophistication and monied supremacy. Its manners and methods had crystallized into disciplined patterns, and woe to the waywards who catered to contrary canons.*

*Families collectively summered at resorts, attended receptions, visited galleries, patronized theaters, and took in sporting events. Whatever happened was planned, proper, and usually expensive.*

*Education was a serious matter. Children attending local grade schools were also subjected to the ministrations of piano teachers and the tyranny of dancing classes. After the grades came private academies for young ladies, with college an improbable luxury. Boys were frequently shipped off to boarding schools whose essential function was preparation*

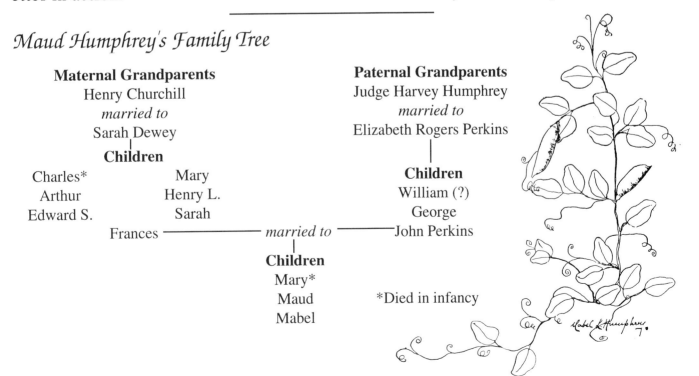

## Maud Humphrey's Family Tree

**Maternal Grandparents**
Henry Churchill
*married to*
Sarah Dewey

**Children**

| | |
|---|---|
| Charles* | Mary |
| Arthur | Henry L. |
| Edward S. | Sarah |

**Paternal Grandparents**
Judge Harvey Humphrey
*married to*
Elizabeth Rogers Perkins

**Children**
William (?)
George
John Perkins

Frances ———— *married to* ———— John Perkins

**Children**
Mary*
Maud
Mabel

*Died in infancy

for acceptance at major universities, Harvard and Yale being primary targets.

As to education, Maud probably attended the same schools as her nurtured contemporaries. Like other little girls she took piano lessons, enrolled in a dancing class and went to Sunday School, in her case at St. Andrew's Episcopal Church, where the instructor was occasionally her uncle George. Church attendance was a social requirement purported to sanctify status and salvage the soul. For Maud, these pretensions paid more in position than piety. Her religion was art.

All was not serious. There was fun with other children. One cheery little incident is recounted. Cousin Joe fell out of an apple tree and broke a leg. Maud came around with a present--something she had swiped from his father's basement--an apple! Eve on Olympus.

While the known facts during this part of Maud's life are few, her family's social and professional connections had brought her in contact with Third Ward activities before she had even moved into her grandparents' house there. She easily fit into the unique lifestyle that was the Third Ward.

Mount Hope Cemetery in Rochester, New York, where both the Humphrey and Churchill family plots can be found. Maud's parents and sister Mary are buried there.

Maud herself was cremated and her remains are at Forest Lawn Cemetery in California.

# CHAPTER THREE
# *Artist in the Making*

*One reason for searching careers of creators is the hope for some clues to their greatness. This is often unrewarding; most geniuses just "came that way." This seems true of Maud Humphrey. There is no evidence of artistic talent or taste in her family background.*

Maud's younger sister Mabel would also become an artist to some extent, but would be known more as an author. At the time of Maud's death in 1940 she was listed as a writer living in New England. Maud and Mabel were the daughters of John Perkins Humphrey who sold stoves, originally working for his brother-in-law's firm and then for his own, John P. Humphrey and Co. Their mother, Frances Dewey Churchill, a relative of Admiral Dewey, ran the household and cared for the children. There had been a third daughter, Mary, born in 1864. However, she died the following August. Another grave next to Mary's at Rochester's Mount Hope Cemetery is simply inscribed "Baby" indicating a fourth child may have been born to John and Frances.

With her inborn talents, Maud must have felt right at home in the artistic environs of the Third Ward and the neighboring "Four Corners" with its Rochester Art Club meetings, the artists corner in the Reynolds Arcade, and The Powers Gallery.

By the 1880s Daniel Powers's art collection had done much to expand the knowledge and appreciation for art among his fellow Rochesterians. Maud inevitably was drawn to the Powers Building and the Gallery it housed to study the paintings, both originals and replicas of the old masters, and to gain insight on technique. She would have learned of her contemporaries there, living artists from both Europe and America were represented in the collection.

Eventually the Powers Gallery exhibited the works of Rochester artists, too. Their numbers grew when a professional art school at the old Rochester Athenaeum and Mechanics Institute commenced. Among the teaching faculty and student body were such artists as George Haushalter, Claude Bragdon, Charles Livingston Bull, and James Hogarth Dennis.

The Reverend James Dennis was a Humphrey family friend. He himself had studied at the National Academy of De-

sign in New York and was the first to give Maud encouragement and basic instruction.

*Maud Humphrey, as an artist, was largely self-taught. Her creative impulses appeared early -- on walls and pillow cases, penciled outlines, mostly of animals. Later she did sketches of neighbor children, including a cherubic seven-year-old A.J. Warner who became a prominent journalist. Others of her models were two sisters, Adelaide and Louise Devine.*

*Formal instruction began when she was a mere 12 years old at evening art classes which she attended during the winters for two years. The classes there were mostly in charcoal drawing. At 14 she received a few lessons in oil painting, two quarters at another city evening school. At this age she was overtaken by a serious visual problem, and for two years she read and painted nothing.*

Whatever the sight problem was, it cleared up entirely, as mysteriously as it had occurred. It was about then that Maud and her family had moved onto Greenwood in the Third Ward. By this time her friend and first art teacher had helped organize the Rochester Art Club. Reverend Dennis became the Club's first president, and Maud was one of the earliest members.

*The Rochester Art Club made efforts to encourage teaching, to coordinate the efforts of various other centers, and to arrange for demonstrations and lectures by well known practitioners, some from abroad.*

Maud would continue to be listed as an exhibiting, non-resident member of the Club long after she had left Rochester. Excluding the 1952 Anniversary Exhibition, the last entry from Maud Humphrey in a Rochester Art Club Show was in 1916.

*Sometime during her formative years, Maud experimented with watercolors. She found this a congenial medium and pur-* *sued it for the rest of her life. Of her watercolor work she later wrote, "What I have accomplished in watercolors has been by study from nature and the occasional criticism of some kind friends among the artists in New York and Rochester."*

In 1886, Maud ventured out of Rochester for New York City to continue her artistic training and foster a career. An early recollection of the Third Ward describes the "going-away process:"

> When you yourself are ready to depart, you receive a volley of nods and smiles and waved hands and shouted adieux that is sure to keep the district dear to your heart however far you travel. But there is a rule, one of those inviolable social laws of the locality, that must be lived up to in departing. You must go away in a carriage.
>
> Perhaps you have regularly walked miles to save fare and think nothing of walking to the station to see a friend; but when you yourself are the traveler, the carriage is necessary.

There's no reason to believe Maud didn't enjoy the same type of send-off from family and friends. Perhaps she had a friend who owned a carriage, but, more than likely, Maud hired one from the local livery to take her and her bags to the station for the trip to New York City and the Art Students League.

*The Art Students League was started in 1875. It was loosely patterned after the "groups," or schools, in Paris and other European cities. It was not, however,*

---

devoted to any single philosophy, fad, or medium. The main purpose of the League was to found and support schools for instruction in all phases of pictorial art. The first such location was in the upper floors of the Weber Building at Fifth Avenue and 16th Street. The rooms were large, the illumination superior, and there were skylights on top.

Members of the League paid dues. Admittance was accorded only to applicants with track records as published artists or demonstrably competent technicians. Classes were conducted by professionals or advanced students, some paid, some not. Though regular periods, or terms, were scheduled, the institution offered no graduation or degrees, but the fact of

An Antique drawing class at the Art Students League around the time Maud Humphrey was a student and member of the Board of Control. While the students are not identified, the woman in the left center bears a resemblence to Maud's self-portrait. *Photograph courtesy of the Art Students League, New York City.*

*having studied there became a respected credential. It must be said of this school that about half of the country's recognized artists were there at one time or another.*

*While in New York, Maud cultivated her fondness for portrayals of children, the specialty that made her famous.*

Records show that in 1886-1887 Maud took "Antique" classes, learning to draw from casts and then to "Life" classes working from live models. There are class records from the Art Students League for Maud through 1894. These classes include painting and sculpting, too.

From its beginning, the League took a much more liberal attitude toward women than did its European counterparts, and included women on its governing board.

The records show that Maud was a member of the Board of Control in 1891, a year before the League moved into the American Fine Arts Building it currently occupies. Again, according to records:

> The Officers ... constitute a Board of Control, to which is committed the entire management of the schools, the transaction of all business, and the furtherance of the artistic and literary objects of the Association.

This Board of Control was elected at annual meetings. Nobody could serve longer than three years except the President. Six people were elected. These six then selected six others to serve with them to make up the 12-person Board of Control. Of these 12, at least four had to be

"Spring Wonder" from *Baby Sweethearts* by Maud Humphrey and published by Frederick A. Stokes & Brothers in 1890.

"You are just a porcelain trifle, 'Belle Marquise,' just a thing of puffs and patches." An illustration from *Poems by Dobson, Locker, and Praed,* Frederick A. Stokes Co., 1892.

Illustrations typical of Maud
Humphrey's early black-and-white work.
From *Grandma's Rhymes and Chimes
for Children*, Roberts Brothers, 1889.

students currently registered at the League. Since Maud's class records go through 1894, it is assumed Maud served as a student member of the Board and served her full three-year term. Undoubtedly this experience in administration helped her in managing her own hectic career later on.

*It is reported that Maud went to Paris after taking courses at New York's Art Students League, but the exact date of this episode is uncertain. Various accounts state that she enrolled at the Julian School and studied privately under Jules Dupre, Whistler and "other masters." In the 1890s Paris was full of masters. Almost cer-*

Illustration for the poem "Little Witches" which appeared in the *Ladies' Home Journal,* November, 1888.

[For The Ladies' Home Journal].
## LITTLE WITCHES.

Grandma says we are little witches,
Make her drop so many stitches;
  Laughing till she fairly shakes
  At our pranks; but she mistakes,
  For when I brought my little basket,
  (Just myself, she didn't ask it),
  To hunt her stitches on the floor,
  (A dozen dropped she said, or more.)
There wasn't one that I could find.
Poor Grandma must be getting blind!

M. M.

This handy booklet published by the Knapp Co. Litho, was distributed compliments of Metropolitan Life. It contains a number of Maud Humphrey images on the front and back covers.

*tainly she encountered the flamboyant Toulouse-Lautrec and Whistler's friend Edgar Degas. Unhappily missing is any hint as to where she lived or how she maintained herself other than by commissions to paint Parisian children.*

Unlike the more prestigious Ecole des Beaux-Arts, the Julian Academy had already opened its doors to women students. Since European techniques were still considered far superior to American, woman artists like Maud now rushed in to take advantage of segregated classes taught by famous French academicians. A letter written by her cousin George during a visit to Paris tells of seeing Maud while he wandered the city. The date of that letter is 1891, indicating Maud went to Paris in between terms at the Art Students League.

*Much has been written - and wrongly-about the "influence" of one artist on another, but a try is forgivable. Maud returned to the States with an improved technique, and the fact of sustained study under Whistler indicates that she found that association valuable. It must have been congenial; both were individualists possessed of sardonic humor, caustic wit, and sharp tongues.*

Maud returned to the States and probably completed a few more classes at the Art Students League. The Julian Academy in Paris and the League in New York gave her the training that brought discipline to her talent and the right techniques of color to go beyond her earlier black-and-white work. Schooling brought her more: romance. The year after attending classes she went a studio reunion. There she met her future husband, Belmont Deforest Bogart, himself from Bath, New York. Events in her personal and professional lives seemed to be falling into place.

**Opposite page:** "First Prayers" from *The Littlest Ones.*

November, 1891.

| Sun | Mon | Tues | Wed | Thurs | Fri | Sat |
|-----|-----|------|-----|-------|-----|-----|
| | | | | | | 1 |
| 1 | 2 | 3 | 4 | 5 | 6 | 7 |
| 8 | 9 | 10 | 11 | 12 | 13 | 14 |
| 15 | 16 | 17 | 18 | 19 | 20 | 21 |
| 22 | 23 | 24 | 25 | 26 | 27 | 28 |
| 29 | 30 | | | | | |

December, 1891.

| Sun | Mon | Tues | Wed | Thurs | Fri | Sat |
|-----|-----|------|-----|-------|-----|-----|
| | | 1 | 2 | 3 | 4 | 5 |
| 6 | 7 | 8 | 9 | 10 | 11 | 12 |
| 13 | 14 | 15 | 16 | 17 | 18 | 19 |
| 20 | 21 | 22 | 23 | 24 | 25 | 26 |
| 27 | 28 | 29 | 30 | 31 | | |

HURRAH FOR THE NURSERY BAND!

## CHAPTER FOUR

# *Career*

Maud's commercial work had begun before she even left Rochester for New York or Paris. The instruction she had up to that point along with her substantial talent was enough to land her commissions for illustrations in children's magazines such as those then associated with the House of Harper and The Century Company. These were black-and-white illustrations. The first of these, for *Our Little Ones,* were made when she was 16.

However, it wasn't until Maud studied in New York and Paris that she fully mastered watercolor painting, the medium for which she would be best remembered. She painted with a watercolor technique so dry as to be akin to etching. Now her career began to take off.

*In one respect, Maud's prompt and popular success was a matter of luck. The*

*immense acceptance of Italian tenor Caruso was due to, in addition to genius, timing. He began his career in America just as Edison's phonograph invaded living rooms with its accompanying standard flat disc recordings of Caruso's renditions of Italian folk songs and operatic selections.*

*For Maud the situation was similar. Her meticulous watercolor technique was ideal for the new methods of colored lithography which changed the looks of books, magazines, calendars, etc. Maud's adorable moppets and winsome misses would help promote such nationally famous products as Ivory Soap, appear in dozens of children's books and magazines, and make their way into every sort of card, from advertising to greeting. She would become the best known illustrator of her time, and the best paid, as well.*

The period in which Maud made her mark is referred to as "The Golden Age of Illustration." This was due to the rapid advancements being made in printing - high-speed presses, half-tone plates which

---

**Opposite Page:** Page from an 1891 calendar published by Frederick A. Stokes and Brother.

**Above:** Illustration from *A Treasury of Stories, Jingles, and Rhymes,* published by Frederick A. Stokes in 1894.

would reproduce any medium including Maud's watercolors, and new four-color printing processes. Now quality books and periodicals could be printed for mass consumption.

And the masses wanted them. Various factors beyond printing technology led to the popularity and success of illustrated publications. First was a general economic stability resulting in a new, prosperous middle class. Also literacy was almost universal among this class which found itself with more leisure time on its hands thanks to shorter working hours and labor-saving inventions.

Many of these same factors, however, also resulted in social changes. The Women's Rights Movement was evolving, which in turn focused on many family issues, such as education, morality, and religion. The heritage of the Industrial Revolution in America included increased immigration and thus more competitiveness, more crowded conditions, and Westward expansion. "Traditional" family life was being threatened.

Not surprisingly, it was "traditional" family values - the home, motherhood, family ties - that became the dominant themes in the increasingly successful periodicals. The illustrations for these periodicals "projected sentiments of security and happiness." So many images spoke of prosperity and security in a country that was outgrowing its age of innocence."

Maud entered the field of illustration when women were, not for any feminist reasons, in big demand. From The Critic: "...Many publishers hold that certain qualities of pictorial interpretation are distinctly the faculty of woman's delicacy and insight to portray." Thus, Maud's charming illustrations of children dressed in Victorian fashions of a gentler era were a publisher's dream come true, and the publisher had become the primary art patron in America.

Because periodicals used illustrations so extensively, readers came to expect these images in their books, too. From

1890 to 1920 illustrated fiction would be an American trend.

So, suddenly the demand for pictures became so large that staff artists were overloaded. Now art editors spent a good deal of their time reviewing portfolios of free-lance illustrators. It was difficult to break in, but once establishing a reputation, an illustrator was seldom out of work.

The demand for good pictures also meant the pay was high. To give a better idea of Maud's popularity, the average illustrator earned $4000 a year, enough for a nice home and a servant. Maud earned $50,000 enough for her family to live in a three-story brownstone in a fashionable New York City neighborhood cared for by four servants.

Among the publishers for whom Maud did work was the Frederick A. Stokes Company who once controlled the right of reproducing her watercolors. The story goes that she had given one of her pictures to a friend who framed it and hung it in the company's store. Officials at the publishing firm immediately recognized the commercial value of Maud's style and sent for her. Her first assignment for them was to illustrate a child's book, and that was just the beginning of a large amount of work Maud did for the Frederick A. Stokes Company.

*In addition to direct publishing, Stokes provided, under contract, an extensive variety of advertising cards, prints and calendars. Among these calendars was a particularly elaborate product known at The Anheuser Busch Art Calendar with appropriate drawings for each season done by Maud Humphrey. This was not a beer ad, but blandishment for a concoction called "Malt-Nutrine," billed as "the most*

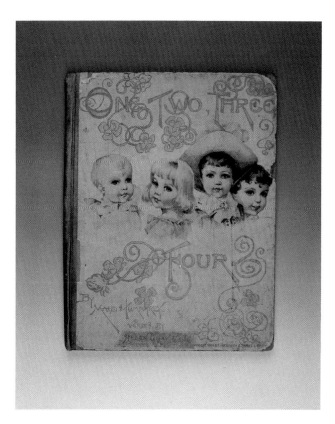

Three books published by Frederick Stokes: *One, Two, Three, Four,* 1889; *Gallant Little Patriots,* 1899; *Children of the Revolution,* 1900.

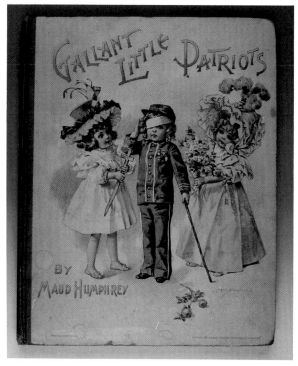

Louis XVI bride from *The Bride's Book*, published by
Frederick A. Stokes, 1900.

| | | | |
|---|---|---|---|
| Rosebud Stories | Holiday | 1906 | $150-$200 |
| Sleepy Time Stories | Putnam | 1900 | $100-$165 |
| Sunshine for Little Children | Sunshine Pub. | 1888 | $150-$175 |
| Tiny Folk/Wintry Days | Stokes | 1889 | $500-$650 |
| Tiny Toddlers | Stokes | 1890 | $575-$775 |
| Vacation Joys | Donohue | | $50-$75 |
| Young American Speaker (with M. Humphrey's "Paul Jones" as full-color frontispiece) | Donohue | | $75-$90 |
| Wildflowers of America | Buer & Co. | | $35-$50 |

## MISCELLANEOUS EPHEMERA

Signed Maud Humphrey postcards and tradecards in pristine condition average $50 to $100 each.

Unsigned cards attributed to Maud Humphrey average $10 each.

Calendars featuring signed Maud Humphrey images average $100 per image and up with prices increasing with the age/condition of the calendar.

The 1906 Art Nouveau calendar for Anheuser-Busch commands $2750 and up.

## CONTEMPORARY COLLECTIBLES

| ITEM | EDITION SIZE | YEAR RETIRED | ISSUE PRICE | CURRENT MARKET VALUE |
|---|---|---|---|---|
| "A Flower for You," cold cast figurine | Membership piece | 1991 membership | | $100 |
| "Cleaning House," 4 1/2" cold cast figurine | 15,000 | 1990 | $33 | $75 |
| "Friends for Life," 4 1/2" cold cast figurine | Members only piece | 1991 membership | | $150 |
| "My First Dance," 4 1/4" cold cast figurine | 15,000 | 1989 | $33 | $250 |
| "Sarah," 4" cold cast figurine | 15,000 | 1989 | $33 | $500 |
| "School Lesson," 5 1/2" cold cost figurine | 19,500 | 1991 | $79 | $150 |
| "Seamstress," 4" cold cast figurine | 15,000 | 1991 | $45 | $400 |
| "Susanna," 4" cold cast figurine | 15,000 | 1989 | $33 | $450 |
| "Tea and Gossip," 3 3/4" cold cast figurine | 15,000 | 1991 | $65 | $100 |

# MAUD HUMPHREY PRICE GUIDE

The ranges of prices in this Guide are based on items in good to excellent condition and reflect current offerings, auction prices, dealers wants and sale prices. If some Humphrey-illustrated publications mentioned in *MAUD HUMPHREY: Her Permanent Imprint on American Illustration* do not appear in this Price Guide, it is due to a lack of current market action on those publications which contain, for the most part, only one or two Maud Humphrey illustrations, usually In black and white.

Special thanks to the following individuals and dealers for help with this Price Guide:
Aleph-Bet Books, Inc.
Jo Ann Reisler, Ltd.
DeeDee Schaeffer
Sarah Steier

## ORIGINAL PUBLICATIONS ILLUSTRATED BY MAUD HUMPHREY

| TITLE | PUBLISHER | DATE | PRICE |
|---|---|---|---|
| Treasury of Stones, Jingles and Rhymes | Stokes | 1894 | $250-$350 |
| Babes of the Nation | Stokes | 1889 | $400-$600 |
| Babes of the Year | Stokes | 1888 | $400-$600 |
| Baby Sweethearts | Stokes | 1890 | $500-$700 |
| Baby's Record | Stokes | 1898 | $250-$400 |
| Bonnie Little People | Stokes | 1890 | $400-$550 |
| Book or Fairy Tales | Stokes | 1892 | $600-$700 |
| Book of Pets | Gardner/Dar. | 1897 | $500-$700 |
| The Bride's Book | Stokes | 1900 | $225-$300 |
| Children of the Revolution | Stokes | 1900 | $500-$700 |
| Children of Spring | Stokes | 1888 | $400-$500 |
| Children of Winter | Stokes | 1888 | $400-$500 |
| Cosy Corner Stories | Hayes | | $100-$150 |
| Cosy Time Story Book | Hayes | | $100-$150 |
| Fun on the Play Ground | Sully | 1891 | $50-$75 |
| Gallant Little Patriots | Stokes | 1899 | $500-$700 |
| Golf Girl | Stokes | 1899 | $300-$400 |
| Grandma's Rhymes and Chimes | Robts Bros.. | 1889 | $45-$60 |
| Light Princess | Putnam | 1893 | $225-$275 |
| Little Colonial Dame | Stokes | 1898 | $50-$70 |
| Little Continentals | Stokes | 1900 | $450-$500 |
| Little Grown-ups | Stokes | 1897 | $500-$700 |
| Little Heroes and Heroines | Stokes | 1899 | $300-$500 |
| Little Homespun | Stokes | 1897 | $100-$140 |
| Little Soldiers and Sailors | Stokes | 1899 | $300-$500 |
| Little Women | Holiday | 1906 | $35-$50 |
| Littlest Ones | Stokes | 1898 | $500-$700 |
| Make Believe Men and Women | Stokes | 1897 | $375-$500 |
| Mother Goose | Stokes | 1891 | $500-$750 |
| Old Youngsters | Stokes | 1897 | $300-$450 |
| One, Two, Three. Four | Stokes | 1889 | $225-$250 |
| Oriana | Estes & Lauriat | 1888 | $30-$50 |
| Playtime Story Book | Hayes | 1891 | $35-$50 |
| Poems by Dobson, Locker and Praed | Stokes | 1892 | $300-$450 |

Colonial bride from *The Bride's Book*.

*nourishing liquid found...which gives health to the weak and ailing." This was sold by both druggists and grocers - no prescription needed.*

While still with Stokes, Maud collaborated with her sister Mabel on two books, *Little Heroes and Heroines* and *Children of the Revolution.* Other Stokes book titles include *Dandelion Time; One, Two, Three, Four; Babes of the Nations; Babes of the Year;* and *Bonnie Little People. The Bride's Book*, published by Stokes strays from the usual children images. However, as the wasp-waisted bride illustrations in this 1904 book attest, Maud excelled at period costuming, especially the Louis XVI and American Colonial periods.

Maud Humphrey's best known publisher was Louis Prang. This famed chromolithographer from Boston popularized the Christmas card in America. Maud had been commissioned by Prang as early as 1887 to draw greeting card designs. Earlier, both in 1881 and again in 1884, she had won prizes in his yearly Christmas card competitions. She also did Valentine designs for Louis Prang and Company.

During this "Golden Age," illustrations were not only found in the pages of America's periodicals and books, but they were what the public chose to hang on their walls. By now, Maud Humphrey was a household name and her paintings household decorations.

A decade after Stokes, Maud worked for the Gray Lithographic Company in New York. Her work for them included frameable prints called "yardlongs," 36 inches long by 8-10 inches wide. From 1880-1910 yardlongs of animals, flowers, and fruit graced many an American parlor. Maud created at least two - "Butterfly Time" (1903) and "Yard of Roses." In addition to "yardlongs," Maud's other big category for Gray was calendar illustrations.

Spawned by the Industrial Revolution, a tidal wave of consumerism flooded America at the turn of the century. The periodical was the perfect place to advertise these goods. Illustrators customized recognizable looks for companies. One of Maud's early advertising successes was for the Mellin Baby Food Company. Using her then infant son, Humphrey Bogart, as a model, she created a highly successful advertising campaign, and, like Maud, the Mellin Baby became a household name.

Magazine advertisers were always looking for new ways to attract potential cus-

**Above:** A young Humphrey Bogart sketched by his mother. Infant Humphrey became the famous Mellin Baby in national advertising for Mellin Baby Food.

**Opposite page:** Gray Lithography calendar for 1908, advertising Wilkie & Platt's clothing store in Amsterdam, New York. These were stock calendars that businesses could buy with their advertising added.

Five calendars from the 1905 Resinol Calendar/Baby Record Book. The sixth calendar top had the same image as the Wilkie & Platt calendar on page 42.

In 1912, the *Farm Journal* used this Maud Humphrey Christmas card design as an enclosure for gift subscriptions.

tomers. Box tops, labels, and wrappers were eagerly collected and then redeemed for illustrator art for the home's walls. Even periodicals themselves offered premiums to new subscribers that could be exchanged for artwork. In 1905 Maud created an art calendar for Resinol that was composed of six leaves with color illustrations on the front and black-and-white sketches on the back that transformed the calendar into a hanging baby record book. A year later her calendar for the Elgin Watch Company featured four panels showing women and watches of various historical periods.

*Between 1875 and 1925 "picturesque" advertising was also done with what were called "Trade Cards" with arresting artistry and the name, product(s) and/or services of the advertiser. Trade cards were mostly cardboard, but occasionally of thin slices of wood, tin or leather. Maud's paintings for these must have run into the hundreds. It's hard to tell since Maud sometimes left such works unsigned, and imitators sprouted everywhere. The same pictures frequently appeared as book illustrations, or vice versa, on calendars and as individual prints for framing.*

*No matter the final form upon which an illustration would appear - book, magazine, calendar, card - art editors worked with very tight deadlines. They favored illustrators who worked quickly, meeting those deadlines, and who had built reputations as specialists. Maud Humphrey was every art director's dream on all these counts.*

Maud's specialty was children's illustrations with an aside in fashion illustration. The latter would play a more important role as her career evolved. She always made deadlines, working deftly in an uncluttered studio. This was indeed quite an accomplishment for Maud. Most of her life she suffered from migraine headaches. Should one besiege her, she knew it meant three days of extreme pain, so she planned her work around this. By the time she would need to ask her doctor husband for medical relief from a migraine attack, she would have already completed whatever

"The Frog Prince" and "Little Red Riding Hood" trading cards were
printed by Gast Lithograph Co. for Woolson Spice Co. A brief outline of
the fairy tale appears on the back.

Maud Humphrey's easily recognizable children appear on
this 1900 calendar for Hood's Sarsaparilla offered as a
premium by C.I. Hood & Co., of Lowell, Massachusetts.

A Maud Humphrey image from an advertising calendar
top for M. Hemingway & Sons Sublime Quality Spool
Silk, circa 1893.

assignment was expected of her.

Much of Maud's work was free-lance. After receiving her assignment she proceeded in whatever way best suited her working habits. She was usually told how many illustrations were needed, color or black-and-white, the page size and format, and possibly what scenes to illustrate. By using freelance artists, the publishers were not responsible for keeping clipping files or for the cost of hiring models.

Maud worked entirely from models. As she herself told a reporter, "My watercolors are done directly from nature, and I usually work

This image by Maud Humphrey appeared on a trade card for the same type of wares her own father had sold in her childhood hometown of Rochester, New York.

them quite dry, and use no opaque color." Undoubtedly, Maud's young models could be paid off rather inexpensively with a few coins or perhaps some treats. And of course, there was always the inexhaust-

ible supply of her own children and their friends.

Despite the benefits of free-lance work, such as the variety of work that expanded an artist's portfolio and, especially for a woman, the ability to stay at home with her family, illustrators were encouraged to take exclusive contracts with top magazines. This insured steady work and security.

So it was that in the second decade of the 1900s, Maud found herself on the staff of *The Delineator.*

*This magazine was almost an arbiter of proper fashion from about 1870 through the 1920s. Starting out as a quarterly in 1872, in was expanded into a monthly in 1875, and so continued until 1935. The stature of this publication can be measured by the reputes of some of its writers, including Theodore Drieser, H.L. Mencken, A.A. Milne, Edgar Wallace,*

Now dollies if you be good we'll have **BROMANGELON** for dessert.

A trade card for Bromangelon, "a powder to produce the most delicious and wholesome dessert jelly in 2 minutes."

*Fall and Winter*          *1902-1903*

OUR HANDSOME NEW

## SUITS AND OVERCOATS

NOW READY FOR YOUR INSPECTION

# KOCH BROS.

ALLENTOWN'S
LEADING CLOTHES MAKERS

This seasonal image by Maud Humphrey appeared on a variety of trade cards.

**Above:** An 1891 image by Maud Humphrey reproduced as a die-cut advertising fan.

**Opposite page:** Maud produced this cover design when she was the Art Director for *The Delineator.*

# The Delineator

**SPRING FASHION NUMBER**

~

*The Newest Styles, the Most Delightful Dresses, Smart Suits and the Newest Accessories*

**APRIL · 1917**

15 cents a copy · $1.50 a year

The BUTTERICK Publishing Company
New York

*John Erskine, Calvin Coolidge and Herbert Hoover. Maud took over at* The Delineator *as artistic director in 1910, a position she kept for the next ten years. During this period she continued to supply hundreds of drawings for the publication, and furnish work to other, noncompeting publishers, as well. It was the busiest time of her life.*

Part of her functions as Art Director of *The Delineator* was choosing the illustrations to match the advance schedule Maud would have been given. The schedule outlined the advertisements, reviews, short stories, and articles by the number of pages of text versus the number of pages of illustration. She also worked on page layout, as well as contributing some of those illustrations herself.

While Maud worked at *The Delineator*, the "Golden Age of Illustration" that had swept her to fame peaked. The year was 1917, and after World War I illustration struggled for awhile and then "succumbed to mediocrity." Entertaining and lighthearted literature was replaced by a trend towards realism that was not well suited to illustration. Just as inventions in the printing processes had given birth to the "Golden Age," another invention, the motion picture, all but killed it. Now another Humphrey was entering the American scene, Maud's son, the actor Humphrey Bogart.

Movies replaced illustrations as the primary visuals for the American public. Radios in every home were the "audio magazines" of the times, dispensing the news and stories. In the periodicals that remained, photography took the place of illustrations. Maud and her fellow illustrators would never again enjoy the popularity they had known from 1890-1925.

By the 1930s, Maud was doing fashion illustration, both for periodicals and for pattern companies like Butterick who had published *The Delineator*. Her faces and figures were still easily recognizable even if the costumes were no longer the Victorian regalia she had used in her earlier illustrations.

Maud was working on these pattern illustrations at that point in her life when her son convinced her to leave New York and join him in Hollywood. What artwork she did there is questionable, although there is one mention of her doing animal paintings. There is also a portrait of Humphrey Bogart from that period, one of only two images this researcher has seen by Maud that is signed with the addition of "Bogart." Was it a testimony to her pride in his achievements, or was she already feeling the obscurity closing in around her, so that she was no longer Maud Humphrey, one of the greatest illustrators in American history, but simply Humphrey Bogart's mother?

WHEN LACE OR EMBROIDERY IS USED ON CHILDREN'S DRESSES, IT SHOULD
BE VERY FINE AND EXQUISITE IN DESIGN

Later in her career, the bulk of Maud Humphrey's professional
work was for fashion illustrations and pattern books.

# BUTTERICK QUARTERLY
## WINTER 1919-1920

Evening Dress for Misses or Small Women 1846     Ladies' Evening Dress 1970     Juniors' Dress 1934     Little Boys' Suit 7581

PRICE 25 CENTS—BY MAIL 10 CENTS EXTRA

WITH CERTIFICATE GOOD FOR 15 CENTS IN THE PURCHASE OF ANY BUTTERICK PATTERN

This Maud Humphrey cover design for *Butterick Quarterly* is one of the few pieces signed with her married name, in this case "M.H. Bogart." Winter, 1919-1920. *Photograph courtesy of the Butterick Company, Inc.*

This sketch of Bogart was drawn by his mother shortly before her death, from a photograph taken when he was a youth. Maude Humphrey Bogart was a noted artist.

While living in California, Maud Humphrey sketched this portrait of her son from a photograph of him as a young man. It is one of the few pieces with "Bogart" as part of the artist's signature. 1938.

*Two Valentines or Florella's Valentine*. A small book published by Art Lith. Publ. Co., Munich & New York. Illustration by Maud Humphrey.

The following pages contain six portraits of young
women from an 1893 calendar. They are a change of
venue from Maud Humphrey's cherubic children.

MARCH 1893

SUN. MON. TUE. WED. THU. FRI. SAT.

|  |  |  |  | 1 | 2 | 3 | 4 |
| 5 | 6 | 7 | 8 | 9 | 10 | 11 |
| 12 | 13 | 14 | 15 | 16 | 17 | 18 |
| 19 | 20 | 21 | 22 | 23 | 24 | 25 |
| 26 | 27 | 28 | 29 | 30 | 31 |

APRIL 189

SUN. MON. TUE. WED. THU. FRI. SA

|  |  |  |  |  |  |  |
| 2 | 3 | 4 | 5 | 6 | 7 | 8 |
| 9 | 10 | 11 | 12 | 13 | 14 | 15 |
| 16 | 17 | 18 | 19 | 20 | 21 | 22 |
| 23 | 24 | 25 | 26 | 27 | 28 | 29 |
| 30 |

MAY  1893

UN. MON. TUE. WED. THU. FRI. SAT.

|  |  | 1 | 2 | 3 | 4 | 5 | 6 |
| 7 | 8 | 9 | 10 | 11 | 12 | 13 |
| 4 | 15 | 16 | 17 | 18 | 19 | 20 |
| 21 | 22 | 23 | 24 | 25 | 26 | 27 |
| 28 | 29 | 30 | 31 |  |  |  |

JUNE  1893

SUN. MON. TUE. WED. THU. FRI. SAT.

|  |  |  |  |  | 1 | 2 | 3 |
| 4 | 5 | 6 | 7 | 8 | 9 | 10 |
| 11 | 12 | 13 | 14 | 15 | 16 | 17 |
| 18 | 19 | 20 | 21 | 22 | 23 | 24 |
| 25 | 26 | 27 | 28 | 29 | 30 |  |

Maud Humphrey

EPTEMBER 1893

MON. TUE. WED. THU. FRI. SAT.
                    1  2
4   5   6   7   8   9
11  12  13  14  15  16
18  19  20  21  22  23
25  26  27  28  29  30

OCTOBER 1893

SUN. MON. TUE. WED. THU. FRI. SAT.
1   2   3   4   5   6   7
8   9   10  11  12  13  14
15  16  17  18  19  20  21
22  23  24  25  26  27  28
29  30  31

November 1893
Sun. Mon. Tue. Wed. Thu. Fri. Sat.

|     |     |     |  1  |  2  |  3  |  4  |
|  5  |  6  |  7  |  8  |  9  | 10  | 11  |
| 12  | 13  | 14  | 15  | 16  | 17  | 18  |
| 19  | 20  | 21  | 22  | 23  | 24  | 25  |
| 26  | 27  | 28  | 29  | 30  |     |     |

December 18
Sun. Mon. Tue. Wed. Thu. Fri.

|     |     |     |     |     |  1  |
|  3  |  4  |  5  |  6  |  7  |  8  |
| 10  | 11  | 12  | 13  | 14  | 15  |
| 17  | 18  | 19  | 20  | 21  | 22  |
| 24  | 25  | 26  | 27  | 28  | 29  |
| 31  |     |     |     |     |     |

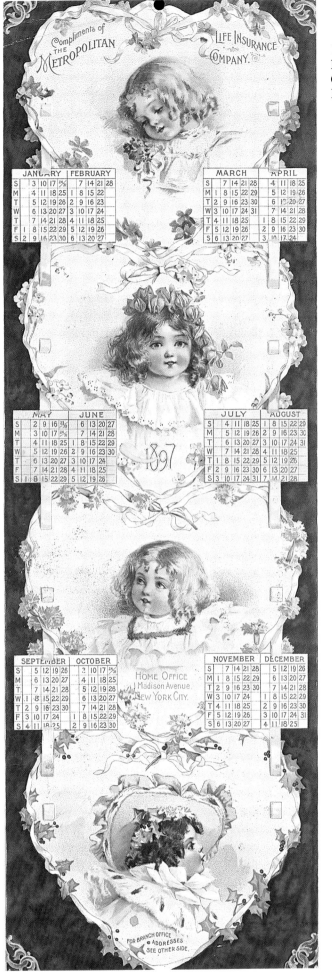

1897 calendar for
Metropolitan Life Insurance
Company. Published by the
Knapp Co., New York.

1898

**Above:** This 1898 calendar page shows the exquisite costuming for which Maud Humphrey was known.

**Page 67 and following:** The following six images were published by the Gray Lithography Company for a 1904 calendar for "The Equitable." They include "Playing School," "Playing Graduating," "Playing Bridesmaid," "Playing Bride," "Playing Mamma," and "Playing Grandma." These same images were reproduced as postcards in 1909 and used in advertisements for K.C. Baking Powder (see page 74).

JANUARY 1904
Sun. Mon. Tues. Wed. Thurs. Fri. Sat.
                              1    2
3    4    5    6    7    8    9
10   11   12   13   14   15   16
17   18   19   20   21   22   23
24   25   26   27   28   29   30
31

FEBRUARY 1904
Sun. Mon. Tues. Wed. Thurs. Fri. Sat.
          1    2    3    4    5    6
7    8    9   10   11   12   13
14   15   16   17   18   19   20
21   22   23   24   25   26   27
28   29

Maud Humphrey - 1902

"STRONGEST IN THE WORLD"

THE EQUITABLE
LIFE ASSURANCE SOCIETY OF THE U.S.
"WORKS FOR YOU WHILE YOU PLAY."

COPYRIGHT 1903, THE GRAY LITH. CO. N.Y.

"Playing School"

MARCH 1904

SUN. MON. TUES. WED. THURS. FRI. SAT.
|   |   | 1 | 2 | 3 | 4 | 5 |
| 6 | 7 | 8 | 9 | 10 | 11 | 12 |
| 13 | 14 | 15 | 16 | 17 | 18 | 19 |
| 20 | 21 | 22 | 23 | 24 | 25 | 26 |
| 27 | 28 | 29 | 30 | 31 |   |   |

"STRONGEST IN THE WORLD"

THE EQUITABLE
LIFE ASSURANCE SOCIETY OF THE U.S.
"WORKS FOR YOU WHILE YOU PLAY."

COPYRIGHT, 1903, THE GRAY LITH. CO. N.Y.

"Playing Graduating"

APRIL 1904

SUN. MON. TUES. WED. THURS. FRI. SAT.
|   |   |   |   |   | 1 | 2 |
| 3 | 4 | 5 | 6 | 7 | 8 | 9 |
| 10 | 11 | 12 | 13 | 14 | 15 | 16 |
| 17 | 18 | 19 | 20 | 21 | 22 | 23 |
| 24 | 25 | 26 | 27 | 28 | 29 | 30 |

MAY 1904

| Sun. | Mon. | Tues. | Wed. | Thurs. | Fri. | Sat. |
|------|------|-------|------|--------|------|------|
| 1 | 2 | 3 | 4 | 5 | 6 | 7 |
| 8 | 9 | 10 | 11 | 12 | 13 | 14 |
| 15 | 16 | 17 | 18 | 19 | 20 | 21 |
| 22 | 23 | 24 | 25 | 26 | 27 | 28 |
| 29 | 30 | 31 | | | | |

JUNE 1904

| Sun. | Mon. | Tues. | Wed. | Thurs. | Fri. | Sat. |
|------|------|-------|------|--------|------|------|
| | | | 1 | 2 | 3 | 4 |
| 5 | 6 | 7 | 8 | 9 | 10 | 11 |
| 12 | 13 | 14 | 15 | 16 | 17 | 18 |
| 19 | 20 | 21 | 22 | 23 | 24 | 25 |
| 26 | 27 | 28 | 29 | 30 | | |

"STRONGEST IN THE WORLD"

**THE EQUITABLE**
LIFE ASSURANCE SOCIETY OF THE U.S.
*"WORKS FOR YOU WHILE YOU PLAY."*

"Playing Bridesmaid"

COPYRIGHT, 1903, 'E GRAY LITH. CO. N.Y.

(over)

JULY 1904
SUN. MON. TUES WED THURS FRI. SAT.
1   2
3   4   5   6   7   8   9
10  11  12  13  14  15  16
17  18  19  20  21  22  23
24  25  26  27  28  29  30
31

AUGUST 1904
SUN. MON. TUES WED THURS FRI. SAT.
1   2   3   4   5   6
7   8   9   10  11  12  13
14  15  16  17  18  19  20
21  22  23  24  25  26  27
28  29  30  31

"Playing Bride"

COPYRIGHT. 1903. THE GRAY LITH. CO. N.

SEPTEMBER 1904
Sun. Mon. Tues. Wed. Thurs. Fri. Sat.
                    1    2    3
4    5    6    7    8    9    10
11   12   13   14   15   16   17
18   19   20   21   22   23   24
25   26   27   28   29   30

OCTOBER 1904
Sun. Mon. Tues. Wed. Thurs. Fri. Sat.
                                   1
2    3    4    5    6    7    8
9    10   11   12   13   14   15
16   17   18   19   20   21   22
23   24   25   26   27   28   29
30   31

Maud Humphrey  1903

"STRONGEST IN THE WORLD"

**THE EQUITABLE**
LIFE ASSURANCE SOCIETY OF THE U.S.
"WORKS FOR **YOU** WHILE YOU PLAY"
(over)

"Playing Mamma"

COPYRIGHT, 1903, THE GRAY LITH. CO. N.Y.

NOVEMBER 1904
Sun. Mon. Tues. Wed. Thurs. Fri. Sat.
    1    2    3    4    5
6    7    8    9    10   11   12
13   14   15   16   17   18   19
20   21   22   23   24   25   26
27   28   29   30

DECEMBER 1904
Sun. Mon. Tues. Wed. Thurs. Fri. Sat.
                        1    2    3
4    5    6    7    8    9    10
11   12   13   14   15   16   17
18   19   20   21   22   23   24
25   26   27   28   29   30   31

"STRONGEST IN THE WORLD"

THE EQUITABLE
LIFE ASSURANCE SOCIETY OF THE U.S.
"WORKS FOR YOU WHILE YOU PLAY"
(over)

"Playing Grandma"

A page from an American Lithographic Co. calendar
copyrighted in 1906 by the Perry Mason Co.

K.C. Baking Powder advertisements, published by Gray Litho. Co., New York. Probably given as a mail-in premium.

**Opposite page:** A cover from the April 4, 1904, Easter issue of *The Sunday Magazine,* with Maud Humphrey's illustration "Easter Morning."

THE SUNDAY
MAGAZINE

CHICAGO, ILL.
APRIL 3, 1904.          SUNDAY RECORD-HERALD          PART 3

COPYRIGHT 1904 BY ASSOCIATED SUNDAY MAGAZINES

EASTER MORNING
by
Maud Humphrey.

A TREE SONG.

Sing a song of Oak trees ;          Sing of this or that tree,
Sing a song of Pine ;               Growing here or there ;
Sing of Elm and Hickory,            All around the world, dear,
Growing broad and fine.             Every tree is fair.
Sing about the Ash tree,            North or South it may be,
Poplar tree and Beech,              Maybe East or West ;
Maple, Birch and Apple tree,        But take them all in all, dear,
Pear and Plum and Peach.            The Christmas tree is best.

"A Tree Song" by Maud Humphrey illustrated a verse that appeared in *Truth* magazine, December, 1900.

BEST
WISHES
FOR YOUR
BIRTHDAY

**Left:** This same birthday postcard image appeared in other forms, such as a 1905 Equitable calendar. Here the image is embossed and guilded on a postcard by L.R. Conwell.

**Below:** Illustration from *Truth* magazine, for "Three of a Kind."

These art prints by Maud Humphrey were for the N.K.
Fairbank Company. On the left is "Evening" and on the
right is "Night." These were offered as advertising
premiums. The reverse sides contain endorsements for
the company's Fairy Soap products from some prominent
Washington women of the day.

Advertisement for Our Pet's shoes. As a child Maud would have worn similar
shoe styles from her maternal grandfather's shoe manufacturing business.

**CHAPTER FIVE**

# *Family*

The following article on the marriage of Maud Humphrey to Belmont Deforest Bogart appeared in the town gossip section of the *Ontario County Times*, June 15, 1898:

A curious story lies behind the marriage of Maud Humphrey to Belmont Deforest Bogart. Miss Humphrey, whose watercolor studies of child-life are familiar to the public, met Dr. Bogart three years ago at a studio reunion. Their engagement seemed imminent but an estrangement followed and for two years the two did not meet. Then came the romance. While doing ambulance work Dr. Bogart broke a leg, but the injury, in some inexplicable manner, was mistaken for a sprain and treated as such. Of course, the limb set itself in a somewhat artless Japanese fashion, and when the young physician discovered what the matter was it became necessary to have the leg broken again and set properly. Here Miss Humphrey appeared on the scene again, and the engagement was renewed.

In view of his impending sufferings, Miss Humphrey thought she would rather nurse her husband through his trial than visit him duly chaperoned at stated intervals, so about the middle of the week the young couple announced

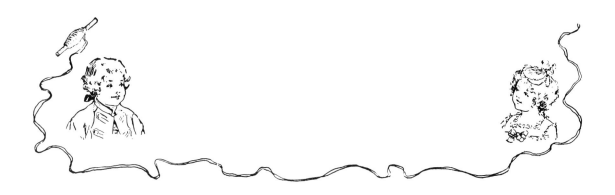

casually that they were going to be married on Saturday, and they were, with only a handful of cousins to give away the orphan artist. The honeymoon will be spent in a hospital. Mrs. Bogart, nee Humphrey, is a connection of Admiral Dewey, and is also related to the Churchills and VanRens-selaers.

Dr. Bogart was just the opposite of his wife. He was easygoing, charming, and casual. Rather than the cultural events, he enjoyed hunting and camping. The Bogart family name has a history. The Bogarts were among the original Dutch settlers of New York, an ancestor being the first European child born in the state.

Belmont Deforest Bogart had inherited a good amount of money that his father had made on the latter's invention of lithography on tin. (How many of Maud's images would find their way onto advertising tins and trays?) With money behind him, Belmont had gone to Andover, Columbia, and Yale. His accident involving the ambulance occurred while he was interning. While it was more than a sprain, it was also more that a simple broken leg as the engagement article would have us believe. The horse-drawn ambulance that had fallen on Dr. Bogart badly damaged his legs and ribs. Some pain would always remain.

Dr. Belmont DeForest Bogart.

Maud Humphrey with infant son and namesake,
Humphrey Bogart.

Dr. Bogart and Maud's first child and only son was born January 23, 1899. Their son was christened with Maud's professional, i.e. maiden name. Early on, it was decided that Humphrey Bogart would attend Yale. The young Bogart family also included two daughters. Francis was two years younger than Humphrey. Her childhood nickname of "Fat" was gradually changed to "Pat." The other daughter, Catherine, was Maud's "favorite."

In the early years of their marriage, Dr. Bogart was a successful physician. He was on the staffs of Bellevue, St. Luke's, and Sloan Hospitals in New York. While his yearly income of $20,000 in those days was less than half that of Maud's, together they supported a fashionable, almost extravagant lifestyle. Of course, in those days the weekly pay for four servants was less than $20.

The young Bogart family lived in a three-story brownstone at 245 West 103rd Street near Riverside Drive. Bay windows looked out on the elegant residential hotel across the street, the Hotel Marseille, where the likes of Sara Delano Roosevelt, F.D.R.'s mother, lived.

Maud's young son, Humphrey Bogart, posed for "The
Surrender of Cornwallis," from *Children of the
Revolution.*

THE SURRENDER OF CORNWALLIS.

Two photos of Humphrey Bogart as a young child.

"Baby's Surprise" from *The Littlest Ones* could easily be mistaken for an image of Maud with her son, Humphrey, and one of his two baby sisters, but it was painted before he was born.

Two maids took care of the horsehair furniture, heavy tapestries, classical statues, parquet floors with their Oriental rugs, and the alabaster and marble trim. They answered the phone, one of the few in the neighborhood. There was also a laundress and a cook.

Their careers allowed both parents to spend a great deal of time at home, but they left the overall care of their children in the hands of others. Dr. Bogart conducted his practice from an office in the family home. This mahogany-lined, green carpeted office was on the first floor. Bedrooms and parlors filled the second floor. On the third floor was Maud's studio and the nursery. A pigeon coop on the roof capped it all off. (Raising pigeons was one of Dr. Bogart's hobbies.) Outside, the latest model car waited to transport Dr. Bogart and Maud in style to Delmonico's or the Lafayette.

On July 5, 1899, Dr. Bogart purchased Willow Brook at Seneca Point, Canandaigua Lake. This would become

Willow Brook, the Bogart family's summer "cottage" at Lake Canandaigua, New York.

Typical of the pastoral scenery around Lake Canandaigua
where the Bogart family summered.

the family's summer "cottage." It more closely resembled an estate. The fifty-five acres included a working farm, ice house, stretches of manicured lawns, and a dock with a sailboat. It was here that Dr. Bogart, the sportsman, taught his son Humphrey how to sail. Sailing became a passion for Humphrey as well. He had a pet mouse, and at Willow Brook he would row out on the lake towing a little raft with his pet on it.

During the summer months at Canandaigua Lake, New York, Dr. Bogart acted as country physician to the locals or "hillers" and to other summer residents known as the "cabin-folk." Maud used the local children as models. One remembered being paid quite handsomely. For an hour's posing, she received a whole dollar. Another child model passed down a story that Dr. Bogart treated patients at Canandaigua free of charge.

Maud's sense of humor was seen throughout Willow Brook. She painted great amusing frescoes on the walls there. However, she could also be temperamental, and more than one of her children's summertime playmates heard her husky voice through open windows shouting at her son and daughters. That, coupled with his father's disciplinary spankings and his mother's arguments against those spankings created memories for Humphrey of a childhood fraught with discord.

Around 1915, the Bogart family sold Willow Brook and took up their summer residence at Fire Island so that Maud could be closer to *The Delineator*'s office where she was now the Art Director. This was not the only change evident in her life.

Arguments with her husband were now a daily occurrence. Often these were over the children, other times she confronted him with what seemed to her his growing disinterest in his practice.

Whether it was her migraine headaches, her big work load, the disintegrating relationship with her husband, or a combination of all these factors, Maud had become even more antisocial. She stayed home when her husband planned outings, seeking sanctuary in her studio.

By the beginning of the Depression, the Bogart family fortune had vanished. Both Dr. Bogart's health and practice were waning. To cope with the chronic pain from his earlier accident with the ambulance, Dr. Bogart had resorted to doses of morphine. For all practical purposes, his medicine had become an addiction.

The family was forced to move from the West Side to an apartment in a converted brownstone at 79 E. 56th Street. It was primarily Maud's art that kept the family solvent. Dr. Bogart took up the periodic job of ship's doctor on small passenger liners. Some say it was to get away from the tense family situation, others that morphine was more readily available to a ship's doctor than a society surgeon.

With the children all grown and gone, Maud and Dr. Bogart moved again. Now they retained two separate flats in the same building. Never losing her sense of

duty and honor, however, Maud took care of her now-bedridden husband to the end. She would sit with him for hours during the day, staying to fix and eat dinner with him in the evenings. She paid for nurses when he required extra care during bad bouts.

Dr. Bogart died in the Hospital for the Ruptured and Crippled in New York in September, 1935. It is said Maud doubled up for a moment as if she had had the wind knocked out of hcr. Then straightening up she said, "Well, that's done." She may have cried alone, but she never broke down in public.

Dr. Bogart left approximately $10,000 in debts which Maud's dwindling commissions could not handle. Their son Humphrey would eventually pay these off with his earnings from the film *The Petrified Forest*.

By now Humphrey was a promising young actor in Hollywood. Though he had been expelled from Andover and never attended Yale, Maud had finally come to accept her son's choice of careers. She even took some pride in his accomplishments. Her daughter Pat had married Stuart Rose who worked for Fox Studios. It was Rose who had gotten his brother-in-law a screen test in 1930.

Pat Bogart Rose became a victim of manic depression that required periodic and increasingly frequent hospitalizations. Eventually she would suffer a nervous breakdown while living in New York. Afterward she moved into an apartment in Hollywood to be closer to Humphrey Bogart and his wife Mayo Methot.

Maud's youngest child died of peritonitis from a ruptured appendix. The medical records point to a weakening caused by heavy drinking. About his baby sister, Humphrey Bogart would tell friends, "She was a victim of the speakeasy era. She burned the candle at both ends, then de-cided to burn it in the middle." Catherine Bogart was only 33 when she died in 1937.

Could these tragic individuals have once been the young models for so many of the happy, carefree children images Maud had painted? How their paths had wandered.

Around the time of Catherine's death, Humphrey finally talked his mother into joining him in Hollywood. Reluctantly she accepted his invitation. At first she thought California a very rough place with no tradition or social background, two elements that always had been key in her life.

Maud questioned the propriety of the apartment her son had gotten her on Sunset Boulevard, even though the luxury apartment house required references. It was at the famous Chateau Marmont, a Hollywood landmark. However, once she saw some of the Hollywood dignitaries in the lobby and outside the grounds of the Marmont - the likes of Laurence Olivier and F. Scott Fitzgerald - she began to feel more at home in a proper social circle.

Maud even began new "traditions." Living close to Hollywood's famous Schwab's Drugstore, she would walk there each day:

> ...as proudly as Queen Mary out for an airing, still erect and wasp-waisted, she strolled the distance to its doors...Schwab's provided her with the activity she missed in retirement. She talked to everyone, made little purchases and then strolled grandly home again.

Maud Humphrey died from cancer in Hollywood on November 22, 1940. The actual cause of death is listed as pneumonia brought on by intestinal obstruction due to a malignant tumor. Her cremated remains were placed in a mausoleum at Forest Lawn, a long way from the

Humphrey burial plot at Mount Hope Cemetery in Rochester, New York.

There were few people left in her life by 1940. Dr. Bogart and Catherine were dead. According to her obituary, she was survived by her daughter Frances (Pat) Bogart Rose, now living again in New York, and her sister Mabel Humphrey Green, as well as her son and daughter-in-law.

The missing and inaccurate information on Maud's death certificate foreshadows the obscurity into which her life would fall. One supposes Humphrey filled out the death certificate as he is listed on it as the "informant." Ironically, although Maud had actively campaigned for women's rights, on her death certificate her occupation is listed as "housewife."

What was Humphrey Bogart's motive for this written "slap in the face," for even in her "retirement" Maud had still been painting? As already noted, Maud took great pride in talking about her family's social standing and heritage, but her own parents had died in the late 1800s. Humphrey's memories of his grandparents and his mother's lineage had faded to blanks like those he left on his mother's death certificate where her parent's names should have been entered.

So ended the career of one of America's greatest illustrators. The canvas of her life had been whitewashed and the events left sketchy at best. Gone was any color of passion, ambition, or success.

The famous Chateau Marmont, in Hollywood, where Maud had an apartment.
*Photograph courtesy of the Chateau Marmont.*

# CHAPTER SIX

# Maud Humphrey's Place in Art History

*The length of time that Maud's career continued was unusual...about 60 years from its Rochester beginnings to its California ending. The number of drawings at a guesstimate of ten a week would come to more than 30,000 and the reproductions a matter of millions. The "Humphrey Baby" became the quintessence of seraphic perfection, a hopeful illusion infrequently found in reality. The sheer skill of these works was their principle wonder. Examples of this are in evidence in books where some of the representations of children are by other artists. The difference is stunning. One asks why these inferior pieces were ever included.*

It may have been luck or fate that Maud Humphrey and the "Golden Age of Illustration" coincided, but it took Maud's talent and perseverance to take her to the top of a long list of illustrators, both men and women, contemporaries like Frances Brundage, Ida Waugh, and Ellen Clapsaddle.

However, finding Maud Humphrey's name in the art history books is difficult. She had two marks against her. First, she was an illustrator; second, she was a woman.

Critics and art historians have long looked at illustrators as the "black sheep" of the art family. However, illustrators have documented life's events with as much insight and have created pieces as emotive as any of the "old masters." Their courses of study are the same and their techniques as exacting as any of the so-called "fine artists."

Even if she was "only an illustrator," Maud's name would appear more frequently had she been a man. She would share the limelight then with the likes of Christy, Flagg, and Gibson.

But just as there was the "Gibson Girl," there was the "Humphrey Baby." It was a look Maud had created that, while others tried to imitate it, could never by equalled. The rosebud lips, the stray curl at the forehead, the bright eyes, and the Victorian costuming all said "Maud Humphrey."

Maud's contributions include a legacy of books that are the epitome of children's illustrated publications. Many times it was her name and not the author's that appeared on the front cover.

She helped make the greeting card an American staple. Her brush and palette promoted advertising campaigns successfully - Prudential Insurance Co., Hood's Sarsaparilla, McLaughlin's Coffee, Ivory.

There are intangible contributions Maud made, too. Since she entered the field of illustration at the beginning of its Renaissance, how many in the following generation of illustrators did she inspire? Dedicated and disciplined, how many art directors did she convince to give another wife-and-mother illustrator a try? How many hearts were made lighter by the charm in her paintings, by an innocence society no longer felt but needed to hold onto in the rapidly changing times? How many Americans made their acquaintance to art through Maud's prints in their homes?

Portrait of Mary Humphrey, Maud's
cousin, painted in 1890.

"My Lady's First Outing" from *The Littlest Ones*.

**CHAPTER SEVEN**

# Collecting Maud Humphrey

Until recently, only a select group of ephemera collectors would recognize Maud Humphrey's name; there has always been that contingent of those collecting Maud Humphrey books, prints, and cards. These treasures do not give themselves up easily.

Prior to 1900, illustrators customarily sold both the drawing and the reproduction rights to a publisher. After the original was photographed, neither the artist nor the publisher had much use for it. Drawings and paintings were sometimes filed away for future use in calendars and advertisement, for example.

Sometimes publishers sold or auctioned off some of these originals in their files. A list of 46 Maud Humphrey works from Prang's own collection of paintings sold at auction, shows that Maud drew at least 18 Valentines, 11 Christmas cards, and 8 Easter cards along with an assortment of floral prints and calendars for the firm. However, most times the origi-

nals were destroyed as publishers periodically cleaned house. It was that practice that makes pre-1900 original illustrations done for books and periodicals so scarce today.

Original Maud Humphrey paintings of any period are harder to come by still. As Humphrey Bogart explained, "Maud never kept her paintings, even the paintings of children. She sold them or gave them away and seemed to feel entirely dispassionate toward them once they were finished."

There are still Maud Humphrey calendars, trade and greeting cards to be found. Her illustrated books command prices in the mid- to upper-hundred dollar range.

Today, however, there is a new group of Maud Humphrey collectors. Rather than the original antique reproductions of her work, a growing number of her fans now search out limited-edition collectibles and giftware based on her artwork. Maud's work is available again on collector plates, music boxes, dolls, and figurines. It is now as popular as it ever was.

In 1988, a major gift and collectibles manufacturer* introduced the *Maud Humphrey Collection* to recreate her be-

---

*Hamilton Gifts Ltd., One Enesco Plaza, Elk Grove, IL 60007

loved illustrations in detailed figurines and gift accessories. The *Collection* premiered with nine cold cast figurines inspired by Maud's watercolor paintings. Each of these original introductions was limited in production to 15,000 pieces. Within five years the *Collection* had grown to include more than 75 figurines and had become one of the most popular collectible lines in the country.

Attesting to the renewed popularity of Maud Humphrey's art, three of the original figurine introductions reached the status of "Edition Closed/Retired" within the first year of availability. Such figurines are now only available on the secondary market. "My First Dance," a figurine of a little girl admiring her reflection in a mirror, became the first figurine to retire in 1989. "Sarah" and "Susanna" soon followed suit.

The distinctive style and appeal of Maud's art enable her admirers and collectors to recall familiar childhood memories that transcend the Victorian era. Her subjects are known for their carefree expressions and the finest attire with plenty of lace, frills, flowers, and wide-brimmed hats.

In 1989 Maud Humphrey collector plates became available.** The *Little Ladies* plates were so popular that two additional subjects were added to the originally planned eight-plate series. The ten issues are "Playing Bridesmaid," "The Seamstress," "The Little Captive," "Playing Mamma," "Susanna," "Kitty's Bath," "A Day in the Country," "Sarah," "First Party," and "The Magic Kitten."

Two of these same subjects are among the favorite Maud Humphrey images captured as figurines - "Playing Bridesmaid," with two girls dreaming of their own wedding day, and "Sarah," portraying Maud's 1898 painting originally entitled "First Day at Worship." The most popular images have been resculpted in the *Petite Collection* of miniature figurines which was introduced in 1991.

That same year a second plate series was promoted. *Victorian Playtime* features "A Busy Day," "Little Masterpiece," "Play-

ing Bride," "Waiting for a Nibble," "Tea and Gossip," "Cleaning House," "A Little Persuasion," and "Peek-a-Boo."

The first "series" of figurines was introduced in 1992. Entitled the *Muse Series*, this collection pays tribute to the fine arts which were known to have been a big part of Third Ward life and which helped shape Maud's own career.

As a fitting tribute to the 125th anniversary of her birth, the *Maud Humphrey Victorian Village* was introduced in 1993 to bring back her carefree days in the fashionable Third Ward of Rochester, New York. The *Village* includes figurines and scenes of the people and places that touched Maud's own life. The scenes include an adaptation of her home at 5 Greenwood.

Maud Humphrey's irresistible children also appear in porcelain bisque figurines. The first made their debut in 1990. Sculpted on a larger scale, these figurines are also limited to 15,000 pieces.

Whether it be a special figurine in a series or another limited-edition piece, all figurines based on Maud Humphrey's art have an annual yearmark or production mark on their underside as of 1992. Yearmarks, which change with the calendar year, indicate to collectors the year a particular figure was made. The first production mark in 1992 was appropriately an artist's palette, symbolizing Maud's love for painting and a career to which she dedicated her life.

In 1991, to meet growing demands, the *Maud Humphrey Collector's Club* was formed.***

*Club* members receive such benefits as a

---

**The Hamilton Collection, 4810 Executive Court, Jacksonville, FL 32216
***Maud Humphrey Bogart Collectors Club, One Enesco Plaza, P.O. Box 245, Elk Grove Village, IL 60007-5401. Phone: 1-708-640-5401

"Dorothy's First Valentine" from *The Littlest Ones.* This is typical of the Maud Humphrey style.

symbol of membership figurine, a *Club* notebook, membership card and a year's subscription to the official *Club* newsletter, *Victorian Times.*

Perhaps this is the greatest indicator of Maud's importance as an illustrator and in the history of American art, that over 100 years after she began her career, people still respond to her art. This test-of-time quality is what makes a classic, and a classic is a touchstone by which all others are judged.

Perhaps, too, that her artwork survives in various forms is the greatest tribute to her career. No matter she is overlooked by the history books or relegated to a footnote, no matter her life story is sketchy in places. She lives on in the few remaining originals, now museum bound, in the antique reproductions so sought after and so dear, and in the contemporary collectibles that once again have made Maud Humphrey one of America's best-loved artists.

Due to Maud Humphrey's popularity her style was often imitated and sometimes plaguerized. The top left image is "A Merry Christmas" from *The Littlest Ones*. The lower image is a Christmas card that "borrows" the image nearly stroke for stroke.

Antimony covered boxes from the contemporary *Maud Humphrey Collection* of gifts and collectibles. *Copyright © Enesco Corporation.*

With renewed popularity in Maud Humphrey, many of
today's figurine reproductions quickly reach Edition
Closed/Retired status. These figurines (left to right),
"Susanna," "Sarah," and "My First Dance," were the first
three to earn this honor and were part of the *Maud
Humphrey Collection's* premiere in 1988. *Copyright ©
Enesco Corporation.*

Among the most popular subjects in the *Maud Humphrey Collection* are "Playing Bridesmaid" and "The Bride." *Copyright* © *Enesco Corporation.*

A miniature collection recreates the most enchanting of the *Maud Humphrey Collection's* subjects on a smaller scale, about one-inch tall. *Copyright © Enesco Corporation.*

Inspired by the sister goddesses in Greek mythology, the
*Muse Series* of figurines was introduced in 1992. "The
Young Artist" is reproduced from an 1897 Maud
Humphrey painting. The same image is part of the
*Victorian Playtime* collector plate series under the title
"Little Masterpiece." *Copyright © Enesco Corporation.*

An adaptation of Maud Humphrey's Third Ward home at 5 North Greenwood in Rochester is part of the new *Maud Humphrey Victorian Village*. The accompanying figurines include a young Maud Humphrey, her sister Mabel, and a neighbor boy, A.J. Warner, whom Maud used as a model. *Copyright © Enesco Corporation.*

**Opposite page:**
Besides figurines sculpted in cold cast, Maud Humphrey images have also been reproduced in porcelain bisque, such as (clockwise from lower right) "Special Friends," "The Bride," "Little Chickadees," and "The Magic Kitten." *Copyright © Enesco Corporation.*

The "Playing Mamma" figurine was created to celebrate the fifth anniversary of the *Maud Humphrey Collection*. *Copyright © Enesco Corporation.*

*Maud*
*Humphrey*
*Bogart*

Collectors' Club

Hamilton Gifts Limited

# VICTORIAN TIMES

*Volume I, No. 6*

*The Official Newsletter of the Maud H...*

## Happy Holidays From

As 1991 draws to a close, we also bring our Maud Humphrey Bogart Collectors' Club to the end of its Charter Year. It has been a year of great beginnings for devoted collectors of the Maud Humphrey Bogart Collection, as the Club has welcomed thousands of you as Charter Members!

This is the season when we tradition... year a... made... At... mal... are...

Y wonderful... war... su... He... ha... fri... an... with e... It h...

you and for us. We have much more about the mag... known as the Victorian... have enjoyed learning a... Humphrey Bogart and... artwork during that time... impossible to read any in-... of Victoriana without disco...

Maud Humphrey Bogart
Collectors' Club
Membership Card

...ship Number: C 91-2937
...on Date: 02/18/92

...ONNA CARUCCI

The *Maud Humphrey Collectors' Club* was introduced in 1991 to give collectors more information about the artist. A one-year membership includes a member-only figurine, *Club* notebook, membership card, *Collection registry*, and a subscription to a quarterly newsletter, *Victorian Times*. Copyright © *Enesco Corporation*.

This delightful Christmas party image was painted in
1894, the same year Maud ended her instruction at the
Art Students League. This image was used for a jigsaw
puzzle.

Maud Humphrey illustrated this sheet music, "She Was a Rosebud," published by American Lithographic Co., New York, c. 1900, and given away by the Kroeger Piano Company, New York. The Music was by Teddy Simonds and the words by Elmer Tenley.

Maud's ethnic illustrations were less stereotypical than most. This image appeared in *A Treasury of Stories, Jingles, and Rhymes* where, again due to Maud Humphrey's popularity, her name, not the author's, appears on the cover.

"Dear Little Japanese Girls," also from *A Treasury of Stories, Jingles, and Rhymes* was published by Frederick A. Stokes Company in 1894 in black and white. A later owner of the book apparently hand-colored some of the book plates.

DEAR LITTLE JAPANESE GIRLS.

Maud Humphrey images from *Golf Girl,* a book
published by Stokes in 1899.

"The Dandelion Chain" is from *One, Two, Three, Four.* This book illustrates Maud Humphrey's popularity. Her name, not the author's, Helen Gray Cone, appears under the title of the book on the cover.

"Hidden Pearls" from *One, Two, Three, Four.*

"Fairy Wine-Skins" by Maud Humphrey from *One, Two,*
*Three, Four*, published by Frederick A. Stokes and
Brothers, 1889.

Frontispiece illustration by Maud Humphrey for *Poems*
by Dobson, Locker, and Praed; published by Frederick A.
Stokes Company, 1892.

Maud Humphrey specialized in period fashion, especially costuming from the Colonial and Louis XVI periods as evidenced in "Betwixt the Paths a Dainty Beauty Stept" and these other illustrations for *Poems*.

"Baby's Roses" from *The Littlest Ones*, published by
Gardner, Darton & Company (London) and written by
Elizabeth S. Tucker.

"First Steps" from *The Littlest Ones*.

Maud Humphrey's 1898 painting "First Day at Worship"
appears as the illustration for "Katie Goes to Church" in
*The Littlest Ones*.

"One Year Old" from *The Littlest Ones.*

"Baby Nan in the Country" from *The Littlest Ones*.

"The Very First School" from *The Littlest Ones*.

"The Cook" from *Old Youngsters* illustrated by Maud
Humphrey and written by Elizabeth S. Tucker, published
by Frederick A. Stokes Company in 1897. The same
illustrations appear in the Gardner, Darton & Company
publication *Little Grown-Ups* in 1897 in England.

"Maternal Cares" from the *Old Youngsters* and *Little Grown-Ups* illustrations.

"The News of the Day" from *Little Grown-Ups*; it
appears on the cover of *Old Youngsters*.

"Calling" from *Old Youngsters*; it appears on the cover of
*Little Grown-Ups*.

Maud Humphrey created the color illustrations like "The Merchant" for *Old Youngsters/Little Grown-Ups*, while the author, Elizabeth S. Tucker, contributed the decorative borders.

"The Physician" as it appears in *Little Grown-Ups*, was painted by Maud Humphrey in 1897. A year later she would marry a physician, Dr. Belmont DeForest Bogart.

"The Seamstress" from *Old Youngsters* and *Little Grown-Ups.*

"Ye Summer Girl" from *Little Grown-Ups* has been
reproduced in figurines and collector plates as "Susanna."

"Tea and Gossip" from *Old Youngsters* and *Little Grown-Ups*.

"Cleaning House" from *Old Youngsters* and *Little Grown-Ups*.

"The Little Golfer" from *Old Youngsters* and *Little Grown-Ups.*

"One, Two, Three - Miss" from *Baby Sweethearts* by
Maud Humphrey and published by Frederick A. Stokes in
1890.

"Bo-Peep" from *Baby Sweethearts*.

"Secrets" from *Baby Sweethearts.*

"A Lecture" from *Baby Sweethearts*.

"Lily" (top) and "The May Basket" (bottom) from *Baby Sweethearts*.

"A Christmas Stocking" from *Baby Sweethearts.*

"Under the Mistletoe" from *Baby Sweethearts*.

"Roosevelt's Rough Riders" appears in *Little Heroes & Heroines* and *Gallant Little Patriots* both published by Frederick A. Stokes in 1899 and written by Mabel Humphrey.

ROOSEVELT'S ROUGH RIDERS

"A Naval Reserve Girl" from *Little Heroes & Heroines* and *Gallant Little Patriots*. It would be a boy, not a girl, in Maud's life to join the Navy, when son Humphrey enlisted years after this 1898 painting was completed.

A NAVAL RESERVE GIRL.

"A Military Band" from *Little Heroes & Heroines* and *Gallant Little Patriots.*

"Wounded Comrades" from *Little Heroes & Heroines* and *Gallant Little Patriots.*

"Hobson and the Merrimac" from *Gallant Little Patriots.*

HOBSON AND THE MERRIMAC.

"Dewey at Manila" from *Gallant Little Patriots*. Maud Humphrey was a relative of Admiral Dewey.

DEWEY AT MANILA.

"Sampson at Santiago" from
*Little Heroes & Heroines* and
*Gallant Little Patriots*.

SAMPSON AT SANTIAGO.

MARTHA WASHINGTON POURING TEA.

"Martha Washington Pouring Tea" is from *Children of the Revolution,* a book written by Maud Humphrey's sister, Mabel. Maud did the book's full-color illustrations while Mabel, an artist in her own right, created black-and-white drawings for this Stokes publication of 1900.

"Washington Crossing the Delaware" from *Children of the Revolution.*

WASHINGTON CROSSING THE DELAWARE.

Like other Maud Humphrey images in the book *Children of the Revolution,* "The Boston Tea Party" was reproduced elsewhere, as in a calendar and postcard series.

THE BOSTON TEA PARTY.

"Paul Revere's Ride" from *Children of the Revolution.*

PAUL REVERE'S RIDE.

"Betsy Ross" from *Children of the Revolution.*

BETSY ROSS.

"Lafayette Dancing the Minuet" from *Children of the Revolution.*

LAFAYETTE DANCING THE MINUET.

"Ben Franklin's Arrival in Philadelphia" from *Children of the Revolution.*

BEN FRANKLIN'S ARRIVAL IN PHILADELPHIA.

"Paul Jones" from *Children of the Revolution*.

PAUL JONES.

"Guinea Pigs" by Maud Humphrey and published by the
Frederick A. Stokes Company in 1893.

Small dogs were in fashion in the late 1800s. This Maud
Humphrey image was drawn to illustrate Elizabeth S.
Tucker's poem, "Dear Puggy." It was published by the
Frederick A. Stokes Co.

One of Maud Humphrey's "Little Bo Peep" images
published in 1893 by the Frederick A. Stokes Co.

This is an example of the type of art print published by the Gray Lithograph Company of New York, circa 1907. These prints illustrated books, calendars, and cards, and can still be found.